Dog Groups

Terrier Group

by Julie Murray

Dash!
LEVELED READERS
An Imprint of Abdo Zoom • abdobooks.com

Dash! LEVELED READERS

Level 1 – Beginning
Short and simple sentences with familiar words or patterns for children who are beginning to understand how letters and sounds go together.

Level 2 – Emerging
Longer words and sentences with more complex language patterns for readers who are practicing common words and letter sounds.

Level 3 – Transitional
More developed language and vocabulary for readers who are becoming more independent.

THIS BOOK CONTAINS RECYCLED MATERIALS

abdobooks.com

Published by Abdo Zoom, a division of ABDO, PO Box 398166, Minneapolis, Minnesota 55439.

Printed in the United States of America, North Mankato, Minnesota.
102023
012024

Photo Credits: Getty Images, Shutterstock
Production Contributors: Jennie Forsberg, Grace Hansen
Design Contributors: Candice Keimig, Neil Klinepier

Library of Congress Control Number: 2023938003

Publisher's Cataloging in Publication Data

Names: Murray, Julie, author.
Title: Terrier group / by Julie Murray
Description: Minneapolis, Minnesota : Abdo Zoom, 2024 | Series: Dog groups | Includes online resources and index.
Identifiers: ISBN 9781098284053 (lib. bdg.) | ISBN 9781098284770 (eBook) | ISBN 9781098285135 (Read-to-Me eBook)
Subjects: LCSH: Terriers--Juvenile literature. | Dog breeds--Juvenile literature. | Dogs--Juvenile literature. | Dogs--Behavior--Juvenile literature.
Classification: DDC 636.755--dc23

Table of Contents

Terrier Group

The Terrier Group has more than 30 dog breeds according to the American Kennel Club (AKC). Most terriers were first **bred** in the United Kingdom.

Scottish Terrier

Russell Terrier

Dogs in the Terrier Group were **bred** to hunt rodents, rabbits, foxes, and racoons.

Some are trained to go into animal holes. They **flush out** the animals.

Characteristics

Terriers are small to medium sized dogs. But don't let their size fool you. They have big personalities!

Cesky Terrier

Airedale Terrier

They can be **feisty**. Some terriers have a hard time getting along with other dogs.

Bull Terrier

Terriers can be stubborn. This can make them hard to train. Gentle and consistent training is important.

American Staffordshire Terrier

Terriers have a lot of energy. They need daily exercise.

Wire Fox Terrier

Most terriers have **wiry** coats. They need special grooming to keep their coats healthy.

Terriers can make good family pets. Proper training and exercise will keep them healthy and happy!

Irish Terrier

More Terrier Breeds

American Hairless Terrier

Dandie Dinmont Terrier

Kerry Blue Terrier

Rat Terrier

Skye Terrier

West Highland White Terrier

Glossary

bred – developed over time for a certain purpose.

feisty – determined or spirited.

flush out – in hunting, to force a bird or other game out of hiding.

wiry – like wire in appearance; thin and stiff.

Index

Online Resources